D1031826

ABOVE GROUND

Also by Clint Smith

How the Word Is Passed

Counting Descent

ABOVE GROUND

POEMS

CLINT SMITH

Little, Brown and Company
New York • Boston • London

Little, Brown and Company
Hachette Book Group
1290 Avenue of the Americas, New York, NY 10104
littlebrown.com

First Edition: March 2023

Little, Brown and Company is a division of Hachette Book Group, Inc. The Little, Brown name and logo are trademarks of Hachette Book Group, Inc.

The publisher is not responsible for websites (or their content) that are not owned by the publisher.

ISBN 9780316543033
LCCN 2022943484

Printing 4, 2023

LSC-C

Printed in the United States of America

For Ariel

Have you ever wondered what it would be like to be a ladybug?

—My son

When I grow up I want to be the sun.

—My daughter

Contents

ABOVE GROUND

All at Once

The redwoods are on fire in California. A flood submerges a neighborhood that sat quiet on the coast for three centuries. A child takes their first steps and tumbles into a father's arms. Two people in New Orleans fall in love under an oak tree whose branches bend like sorrow. A forest of seeds are planted in new soil. A glacier melts into the ocean and the sea climbs closer to the land. A man comes home from war and holds his son for the first time. A man is killed by a drone that thinks his jug of water is a bomb. Your best friend relapses and isn't picking up the phone. Your son's teacher calls to say he stood up for another boy in class. A country below the equator ends a twenty-year civil war. A soldier across the Atlantic fires the shot that begins another. The scientists find a vaccine that will save millions of people's lives. Your mother's cancer has returned and doctors say there is nothing else they can do. There is a funeral procession in the morning and a wedding in the afternoon. The river that gives us water to drink is the same one that might wash us away.

Waiting on a Heartbeat

the doctor says you are there
even though we cannot hear you

and you know what they say about the tree
falling in the forest

and i know i have never heard a tree
i could not see

but i have seen trees i could not hear
little one

they tell me you are half the size of a fingernail
and when i hear that i look down at my cuticles

and imagine you sitting there
telling me dad it's going to be okay

there is nothing
to worry about

there is joy in being
a father to a mystery

there is grace in observing the tulip
and knowing it will not bud before your eyes

little one

you are my daily reminder

that you do not go to a garden to watch

the flowers grow

you go to give thanks

for what has already bloomed.

FaceTime

On another night
in a hotel
in a room
in a city
flanked with all
that is unfamiliar
I am able to move
my finger along
a glass screen
once across
once vertical
and in seconds
see your mother
smiling in our room
that is both so far
away and so familiar
in the cradle
of my palm
and she can place
the small screen
near her belly
and when I speak
I can see you
moving beneath
her skin as if you
knew that this

distance was

only temporary

and what a joy it is

to be somewhere

that is not with you

but still with you

and see your feet

dance beneath her

ribcage like you knew

we'd be dancing

together soon.

Passage

Tonight I read you Dr. Seuss
as we do each evening and my mouth
contorts over amorphous letters
while your mother laughs at my blundering
tongue. But I'm not sure I'm to blame
for fumbling over *Circus McGurkus*
and *Yertle the Turtle*. It's just that sometimes
it can feel sort of silly because I have
these moments where I look down before
I flip the page and realize that I am talking
to your mother's skin—
well not her skin, per se,
but the half-globe of your yet-born body
swimming beneath it. I read a sentence
and watch you kick, and I tell your mother
that you are laughing and she tells me you
are trying to let me know that my turtle
voice is subpar. I try a new version,
less nasally, higher pitched,
and you kick as if to tell me just to finish
the book already, you're trying to go to sleep.

"It's All in Your Head"

When your mother was five months pregnant she told me her feet were itching, so I rubbed lotion across their arches as she continued to carry the weight of you. The next day she told me her feet burned, a bed of untamed embers, so we soaked them in cold water until her skin pruned and her heart tempered its restless pulse. The next night she woke me and said the heat was crawling up her legs, so we called the nurse, who told us to come in right away. When we arrived, they hooked her to machines that rang with a desperate hum. We waited for one hour and then waited for several more. When the doctor finally arrived, he looked at the clipboard he had been handed. He checked several boxes. He scribbled through lines. He looked up. He smiled. He told us everything was fine. He said we should go back home, that we really shouldn't worry, that it was likely psychosomatic and something that would go away with time. Your mother took a deep breath—an eruption hidden behind the blanket of its own ash. She asked the doctor if he would please run some tests so that we could be absolutely sure. The doctor shook his head, lifted his hand, and swallowed all of the sound in the room: *Sometimes during pregnancy, symptoms arise that don't mean much and sometimes the problem is all in your head.* He walked out of the room and told the nurse to send us home. But the next day the heat in your mother's legs grew into a blaze. We drove back to the hospital and asked to see a different doctor. The nurse said that wouldn't be possible. Your mother's restraint fractured. She has never allowed someone to tell her the ground isn't there when she feels its soil beneath her feet. She leaned over the desk: *I am not asking you, I am telling you, I need to see a different doctor.* The nurse, now anxious, disappeared into the hall. We were called to see a different doctor and that doctor ran the tests that your mother asked for. What she found occurs in one out of one thousand pregnancies. She told us you need to be delivered early, that waiting too long might mean you extinguish in a womb of poisoned blood. I keep thinking of what could have happened, of what almost did.

Trying to Light a Candle in the Wind

Each evening, ever since the doctor told us
how uncertain you were, your mother lifts
her shirt and rubs Vaseline around her navel,

her two fingers moving in circles across her
growing, gorgeous belly. We put the doppler
to her skin, its cool surface sending goose bumps

across her body. I place the small headphones
in my ear and listen as you somersault back and forth
between the walls your mother built for you.

I am here, I feel you say. *I am still here.*

Your mother and I smile a mix of joy and relief
and marvel at all that you have already given
us. Our lives, an endless procession of doctors'

appointments and lab tests and moments
just like this one. But some days, I worry
that we are welcoming you into the flames

of a world that is burning.
Some days, I am afraid that I am
more kindling than water.

When People Say "We Have Made It Through Worse Before"

all I hear is the wind slapping against all the gravestones
of those who did not make it, those who did not
survive to see the confetti fall from the sky, those who

did not live to watch the parade roll down the street.
I have grown accustomed to a lifetime of aphorisms
meant to assuage my fears, pithy sayings meant

to convey that all ends up fine in the end. But there is
no solace in rearranging language to make a different word
tell the same lie. Sometimes the moral arc of the universe

does not bend in a direction that comforts us.
Sometimes it bends in ways we don't expect and there are
people who fall off in the process. Please, dear reader,

do not say that I am hopeless. I believe there is a better future
to fight for, I simply accept the possibility that I may not
live to see it. I have grown weary of telling myself lies

that I might one day begin to believe. We are not all left
standing after the war has ended. Some of us have
become ghosts by the time the dust has settled.

By Chance

If the doctors said you were impossible and
you arrived anyway does it mean they were

wrong or does it mean you defied science?
What is the difference between science

and a miracle other than discovering new
language for something we don't understand?

The day we brought you home I stayed up all
night and watched you sleep in your bassinet because

I was afraid if I closed my eyes you'd vanish.
Once, a long time ago, your grandmother escaped a war

and your great-grandfather fought in one—you come from
good fortune—you come from a history that is arbitrary

and cloaked in luck—you come from a land
mine that was two feet to the left—

you come from children who shared their bread when they didn't have
to. You come from the parachute that didn't open then did.

In the Grocery Store You Are Wrapped Tightly onto My Chest

in a cloth that is sturdy enough to secure you but flexible enough to let you breathe without straining   we are perusing the cereal aisle and they are playing Stevie Wonder over the loudspeakers   which I didn't realize is something grocery stores did   I mean I guess I didn't realize they played music at all   I mean I didn't realize they could turn aisle seven into a soul train line of Cinnamon Toast Crunch and Apple Jacks   and at first I was just going to nod my head to *Songs in the Key of Life*   but who are we not to take full advantage of this small moment of funky glory   so I wrap my right foot behind my left and spin my body like David Ruffin taught us and when I come back around I see you looking at me saying   *dad is that all you got?!*   and you don't use those words exactly because   you have not yet learned how to speak   but I can tell by the way your eyes widen and your mouth hangs ajar that you are telling me I need to step it up   so I take up your clarion call   and push the shopping cart aside   I grab the maple syrup from the shelf   and turn aisle seven into a medley of Motown throwback moves   spinning and dipping around the oatmeal   bopping among the Froot Loops   moonwalking past the pancake mix   I mean we turn the space between Pop-Tarts and Quaker Oats into Showtime at the Apollo   and after what seemed like hours of loosening our appendages to the beat   I look down to see the swell of your plump cheeks and know that you are proud   and it is then that I look up   and see a store employee staring at us from the end of the aisle   and I am sure she is about to burst into applause because how can you not be impressed by the swift pirouette of a father and son and your favorite box of cereal   and though she does not clap   and though she seems to have called the manager   and though he comes over to say   *sir we appreciate your patronage but your sudden movements are keeping other customers from purchasing their breakfast*   we know we have put on a show   the people will never forget.

Ode to the Electric Baby Swing

When we first met, I wasn't
really thinking I needed someone
like you. But a friend told me that
we'd be a good fit especially with
everything happening in my life.
All the changes, all the uncertainty.
He said it would be nice
to have someone you can count
on. He said he used to have someone
just like you. So, while I think he and I
have slightly different tastes, I thought
it couldn't hurt if we at least had
the chance to meet, and my wife said it
might be nice to introduce something new
into the fold, which left me a bit
confused by how receptive she was to the
possibility of you, I mean she was never
this open to throwing new things into
our relationship before, but I digress. So
anyway, I agreed and when you first showed
up at my door you didn't look anything
like you did in the pictures I saw online.
You came so broken and in so many
different pieces, which left me worried
because I wasn't looking for a project.
I need to focus on my career, you know?

But you were already here and I was raised
to have manners. So you came in and we sat
together on the floor. I put on some
smooth jazz and I helped you put yourself
back together the best way I knew how.
And man, am I glad we got past that first
awkward stage because now you are
the best thing that has ever happened
to me. I literally cannot imagine my life
without you. The moment I handed
you my son he fell asleep in your hold
and I danced in the living room because
before he refused to sleep, but now
he sleeps when you hold him, and my wife
thinks I love you more than I love her
and I'm not saying she's right but I'm not
saying she's wrong, but I am saying you
give me something she doesn't, and don't
get me wrong I love the mother of my son
it's just that you make me feel young again.

Ode to the Infant Hiccup

You small dollop
of untamed oxygen.
You follow no rules
and you never arrive

alone. A spontaneous
wave of soft spasms
rolling across my baby's
chest. You are adorable

until you wake the sleeping
child, until the
unprompted convulsion
of a new diaphragm shakes

the bassinet to life. You
are the small brewing of
thunderstorms inside a
pair of fragile lungs, an

unpredictable quake after
the bottle has injected pockets
of air into this little frame,
an intermittent reminder

of how our bodies have
always been inexplicable
vessels of energy we can
not control.

Ode to the First Smile

At first, I wasn't sure if it had really happened—
perhaps my eyes were wishing for something
that wasn't there. But then you did it once more,

as if to remind me I shouldn't doubt the creasing
of your small eyes, the soft crescent of your
flowering mouth unfurling at the edge.

It happens as I am reading you a story
about a turtle who spends each day going
on adventures with other creatures of the sea

and as I read the turtle's conversation with his dear
friend the octopus—suffused with jokes of seaweed
and tentacles and how coral reefs always stay up

beyond Christmas—you lift the borders
of your mouth and swing your arms in delight.
The haters say it's too early, that it was probably

only gas and the spasms of new muscles.
But we know better than to explain away
such rejoicing. Besides, only 1 in 1,000 baby

sea turtles will survive into adulthood, and we are reading
about one of them, and he is talking to an octopus, and they
are making homophonous jokes about the winter holidays,

and what a glorious example of a miracle this is. So why
would we not praise this flesh and all its fledgling
movements? Why would we concern ourselves

with *how* the turtle arrived in the water
when we could simply celebrate the fact that it
is swimming safely out at sea?

Nociception

When one of the arms of a longfin squid is sliced off
by the pincer of a crab, or snapped away by a fish
who seeks to turn its appendage into sustenance,
the squid does not feel pain in its injured arm
but experiences the sensation of discomfort
across its entire body. It is as if you got a paper
cut on your finger and felt all of your skin
become delicate, hypersensitive to touch.

You, little one, are not attached to my body,
you are neither a limb nor a slice of skin,
but you are part of me in ways I am still
discovering, and when you are hurt, I feel
your distress spread through every cell in me.
I experience your wounds as if they were my own.

Your National Anthem

Today, a Black man who was once a Black boy
like you got down on one of his knees and laid
his helmet on the grass as this country sang

its ode to the promise it never kept
and the woman in the grocery store line in front
of us is on the phone and she is telling someone

on the other line that this Black man who was once
a Black boy like you should be grateful we live
in a country where people aren't killed for things like this

you know, she says, *in some places they would hang you*
for such a blatant act of disrespect, maybe he should
go live there instead of here so he can appreciate what he has

then she turns around
and sees you sitting in the grocery cart surrounded
by lettuce and yogurt and frozen chicken thighs

and you smile at her with your toothless-gum-smile
and she says that you are the cutest baby she has
ever seen and tells me how I must feel so lucky

to have such a beautiful baby boy and I thank her
for her kind words even though I know I should not
thank her, because I know that you will not always

be a Black boy but one day you may be a Black man
and you may decide your country hasn't kept
its promise to you either and this woman, or another

like her, will forget you were ever this boy and they
will make you into something else and tell you
to be grateful for what you've been given.

For Willie Francis, the First Known Person to Survive an Execution by Electric Chair, 1946

Seventeen.
Black boy.
Tied down.
Both arms.
One leg.
Head placed.
In bag.
Tears flow.
Wet face.
Soft skin.
Mouth shut.
Eyes closed.
Heart beats.
Strapped tight.
Heads bend. Prayer said. Flips switch. Boy yells.
Flips switch. Boy screams. Flips switch. Boy still.
They think. Boy dead.
Boy breathes. He lives.
Just one. More year.
Boy says. Please help.
They say. We can't.
He is. Sent back.
Same chair. New sky.
They try. Again.
They do. Not fail.

Roots

Your great-grandfather was born in 1930 Mississippi.
You were born five months ago in Washington, D.C.
Your life is only possible because of his ability
to have walked through this country on fire
without turning into ash.

You come from his deep voice,
you come from his thick bones,
you come from the curl of his Ls
when he says hello.

The first time I handed you to him, I watched
as you settled on his lap. I saw the way your brows
furrowed just like his, how your eyes carry the same
pools of wonder, how when both of you smile it begins

on the left side of the mouth and then blooms
into chrysanthemums at each edge.

Across Generations

So much of what I've learned about being
a father I learned from my father,
and so much of what my father learned

of raising children was pulled
from the spaces between his father's name.
My grandfather's father was a man

whose name I can't remember, but I wonder if his rage
is the ammunition trying to make a weapon
of my voice. When I speak to my son I carry

the echo of generations. Of men attempting
to unlearn the anger on their father's
tongues, the heat in their hands.

The Drone

the drone was once a scrap of metal   the drone looks as if it might be a toy   the drone is not a toy   the drone could have been something else something other than a killing machine   the drone could have been a house   the drone could have been a spoon   the drone could have been a swing   the drone does not know who it is going to kill next   the drone is going to kill next   the drone has learned to disguise itself as a shard of sky   the drone's hum is a disembodied echo   the drone was mistaken for a star once   the drone renders itself celestial   the drone scoffs at sovereignty   the drone asks   *what is a border if you can fly right over it?*   the drone was built by a man   the drone killed a man   and a woman   and a child   the drone killed a child   and did not see her face the drone does not see a face   the drone sees a body   and then the body is gone

Pangaea

Imagine each continent a splintered
tessellation of wayward fragments.
Each mass of land attempting

to jostle itself free. Pangaea was the last
of the supercontinents, a mass of land
that came together and broke itself apart

several times before. It should come
as no surprise; don't we all
eventually return to something

we can lose ourselves inside of? Can we
blame the desert for missing the breeze
that tumbles across the grassland?

Can we blame the tundra for its desire
to witness the wrestling of pines? Just
the other day, a bomb killed seventy people

across the sea and no one around me
heard a sound. These days, I find myself
blaming Pangaea for the sounds I cannot

hear. I decry the continents for their careless
drift. I detest the tectonic plates
for their indifferent quake. I wake up in love

with the ocean and fall asleep despising
all it has put between us. Perhaps if the
continents had never shaken themselves

free we might find ourselves
disabused of this apathy. Perhaps
if we could hear the bomb dropping,

we might imagine what would happen
if it struck our own homes. I am nostalgic
for a proximity that may not have mattered.

I find myself loathing a miracle.

The *New York Times* Reports That 200 Civilians Have Just Been Killed by U.S. Military Air Strikes

and the man on television calls it
unfortunate yet inevitable collateral damage.
And I wonder what it is that turns mourning into a metonym
or a proclamation of conjecture.
And I read his bio and see that he has a wife
and I can't imagine he would call it inevitable
if her body were pulled from the rubble.
And I see that he has a son
and I can't imagine he would call the boy who bears his name
collateral in someone else's war.
And I see that he has a daughter
and I think of what it might mean for someone
to render her final breath an inevitability of realpolitik.
And I understand what he means.
I know he means that war is callous and unforgiving,
that a militant can surround himself
with a dozen women and children
so that the pilot must decide between a target
and the ache of his own heart's detonation.
I do not misunderstand the cruelty of war
but I regret the way we talk about its casualties,
how their lives become tacit admonitions,
how the tyranny of a border made out of thin air
means bombs are only dropped on one side of it.
But I too have felt empathy corrode inside

my most cavernous parts,

have taken the quarters from my pocket

and used them to cover my collusion.

Who among us has not used spare change

to cover our contrition?

Or laid a wreath of sympathy

atop bodies with names we do not know?

I'm not sure what it means for us,

not to be the one to fire the bullet

but to behave as if the bullet always belonged

in that chest, and not our own.

The Great Escape

The first time we bought a baby monitor I was reluctant
to set it up. With all the stories of how the government
is watching us through our laptops, listening to us through
our speakers, and tracking us through our phones, the last

thing I thought we needed was to bring another means
of surveillance into our home. Ultimately, I relented, if
for no other reason than to mitigate my fear that you
would somehow fall out of your crib. Every night

I put you down, turning the bedtime routine
into a Broadway musical like I was auditioning for *Hamilton.*
I mean we got the bath-time song, the toothbrush song,
the pajama song, the no you cannot have any more

Ritz crackers song, the please don't reach down
and touch your poop while I am changing you song.
All the classics.
And even after my ballads, after I kiss your head and cup

your cheeks, each night I watch from the baby monitor
as you attempt an elaborate escape effort. You think
you're slick, but I see you. Each time I leave the room
and turn off the light, you immediately turn to your sinister

co-conspirators, Leo the Lion and Porkchop the Puppy,
to devise a plan on how to escape the crib and forge
a path to freedom. Your mother and I watch on the small
black-and-white screen from the kitchen downstairs as the three

of you huddle together in the corner of the crib to concoct
the evening's plan. There was the time you stripped off
your bedsheet, tied it together, handed it off to Leo,
and asked him to hold one end of the knotted sheet while

you used the other end to rappel down the side of the
crib. It was unclear how much this had been thought out,
and Leo understandably looked terrified, but fortunately
for him your thumb and index finger dexterity had not yet

fully developed so you couldn't tie the knots in the first place.
Then there was the time you realized that we could see you
through the monitor. So you stared right into the camera,
narrowed your eyes, lifted Porkchop over your head,

howling an indiscernible cry toward the heavens, and threw
the stuffed puppy out of the crib and toward the monitor—
a plan it seemed unclear that Porkchop himself
had consented to—as his floppy ears somersaulted

across the room. You missed the camera completely,
as you are a toddler with poor aim and little hand-eye
coordination, while Leo crawled to the corner of the crib,
hoping he would not be your next aerial sacrifice.

Nomenclature

Your mother's mother came from Igboland
though she did not teach your mother her language.
We gave you your name in a language we don't understand
because gravity is still there
even when we cannot see it in our hands.

I ask your mother's mother to teach me
some of the words in hopes of tracing
the shadow of someone else's tongue.

The same word in Igbo, she tells me, may have four different
meanings depending on how your mouth bends around
each syllable. In writing, you cannot observe the difference.

The Igbo word *n'anya* means *sight*
The Igbo word *n'anya* means *love*

Your grandmother said,
I cannot remember the sight of my village
or
Your grandmother said,
I cannot remember the love of my village

Your grandmother's heart is forgetting
or
Your grandmother's heart is broken

Your grandmother said,

We escaped the war and hid from every person in sight

or

Your grandmother said,

We escaped the war and hid from every person in love

Your grandmother was running from danger

or

Your grandmother was running from vulnerability

Your grandmother said,

My greatest joy is the sight of my grandchild

or

Your grandmother said,

My greatest joy is the love of my grandchild

Your grandmother wants you present

or

Your grandmother wants you home.

This Is an Incomprehensive List of All the Reasons I Know I Married the Right Person

Because on weekends you wrap your hair with a scarf
and you have so many different scarves that come in
so many different colors and now when I'm out in the world
every time I see a colorful scarf I think of you and I think
of the weekends which are the best days because they are
the days that you and I don't have to worry about work
or deadlines just bagels and bacon and watching this small
human we've created discover the world for the first time.
Because when you laugh you kind of cackle, no I mean you
really cackle like you take a deep breath in and out comes
something unfiltered and unrehearsed and it's cute
but also scary and isn't that the perfect description of love?
Because when you watch *The Voice* you talk to the judges
as if they are waiting for your consultation. Because you
always ask the restaurant to make your pizza extra crispy
and then you put it in the oven for another thirty minutes
anyway after they deliver it. Because when you wake our son
up in the morning you are always singing. Because when
I read you poems I love you always close your eyes
and tell me your favorite line. Because on my birthday
you had my friends make barbecue and we had leftovers
for weeks. Because I like my cinnamon rolls
with maple syrup and honey mustard and you still kiss me
in the morning. Because you hold my hand
when I'm scared and don't know how to say it.

Lines in the Sand

Yesterday, a boat—carrying too many—capsized at sea on its way
to new land. Yesterday, there were children in cages at the border
stripped from the arms of their parents as they slept at night.

Why is the site of so much violence often an imagined thing?
Not the blood, but all it washes over. Someone stepped
over a line in the sand and it was called a war. Someone spilled

history in the ocean and it was called treason. Someone handed me
an envelope and called it safety. Someone gave me a passport and called it
home. I was born onto a sheet of paper and became a citizen of a lie.

And the World Keeps Spinning

Over the course of 350 years,
36,000 slave ships crossed the Atlantic
Ocean. I walk over to the globe and move

my finger back and forth between
the continents. I try to keep
count of how many times I drag

my hand across the bristled
hemispheres but grow weary of chasing
a history that swallowed me.

For every hundred people who were
captured and enslaved, forty died before they
ever reached the New World.

I pull my index finger from Angola
to Brazil and feel the bodies jumping
from the ship.

I drag my thumb from Ghana to Jamaica
and feel the weight of dysentery
make an anvil of my touch.

I slide my ring finger from Senegal
to South Carolina and feel the ocean
separate a million families.

The soft hum of history spins
on its tilted axis. A cavalcade of ghost ships
wash their hands of all they carried.

Tree Rings

City Park in New Orleans has one of the largest collections of live oaks in the world. Over a thousand acres of forest sitting at the edge of uptown with streetcars tracing its outline like a parade of new moons. On the southeast side of the park, past the botanical garden, over the old bridge, near the elbow of the little lake where the geese hold court, is the tree my mother used to take us to. How I loved this tree. How its branches bent down to the soil as if it had long been waiting to scoop us up. How the Spanish moss tickled my bare ankles as if trying to make me laugh. How, if you stepped back and squinted, the tree looked like a tangle of dragons frozen mid-dance. We had no way of knowing how old the tree was, but my mother used to say that this tree had been at the park since she was a little girl, and that we were climbing the same branches she and her siblings had climbed all those decades before. I found comfort in this story, that something had sprouted from the soil that I shared with the little girl my mother once was. I could close my eyes and imagine climbing with her—swinging our legs, fingers clinging to the soft bark, waiting to see who would fall first.

Here Nor There

I have tried to write these poems before, you know, the ones about the infamous storm and its majestic violence. The floodwater that swallowed a city then sat still as night. I think often of the things it took from us that we'll never know we could have had. Nostalgia is a well-intentioned wound. Counterfactuals are a bed of thorns in a room with nowhere else to lay your head. I imagine what could have been but never was. The Christmases with my children in the home where I once opened presents. Kicking a soccer ball with my daughter against the same playground wall where I imagined a life of goals and glory. That home is now silent as a sky of smoke. That wall is no longer a wall, but a pile of wood in a lonely field. I tremble at what I already know, that my children will not know this city beyond the holidays and funerals that bring them here. That I no longer know the city I have always worn like a tattoo. I still remember the city as something it was kept from becoming. I am still looking for a language not covered in mud.

At the Superdome After the Storm Has Passed

A helicopter hovers overhead like a black cloud of smoke,
its blades dismembering the pewter sky. Men in uniform
stand outside with guns nested under their arms and the hot,

wet air of August licking their weary faces. Two women push
a homemade raft through warm brown water that rises up
and hugs their chests. There is an old man inside the raft who

was once a stranger to them, when such a word meant something
other than *please help me.* Inside, children are running
across the emerald turf, jumping through rings of light that spill

from the sky onto the field. Their small bodies sprinting
between the archipelago of sprawled cots. There is a mother
who sits high in the seats of the stadium rocking her baby

back and forth, her voice cocooning the child in a shell of song.
Before desperation descended under the rounded roof,
before the stench swept across the air like a heavy fog,

before the lights went out and the buses arrived, before the cameras
came inside and showed the failure of an indifferent nation, there were
families inside though there were some who failed to call them

families. There were children inside though there were some who
gave them a more callous name. There were people inside
though there were some who only saw shadows.

It Is Halloween Night and You Are Dressed as a Hot Dog

Why we have chosen to bundle you into a costume
of cured meat I do not know. But your mother
is dressed as a pickle and I am dressed as a bottle
of ketchup and together we make a family of ballpark
delicacies. You have yet to eat solid foods but after
you look at yourself in the mirror you begin to chew
on your costume, clearly compelled by this mystery
mix of pork and beef and purée of other unknown
meats. We place you on the couch next to a large
stuffed bear in hopes of taking photos to send
to your grandparents, because who are we to deny
anyone the joy of an infant wrapped in processed meat.
But you are just a few months old, and thus unable
to sit up straight for very long. So you fall over
onto the lap of the bear, and your mother and I look
at each other, realizing the perfection of what has
appeared before us. So we snap a dozen photos
of the stuffed bear eating the human-hot-dog-baby
(which sounds unsettling but is actually adorable)
and send them to the family group chat right away.
You are probably annoyed, but we are delighted,
and it doesn't even matter if we make it out of the house
anymore because the mission has been accomplished.

When We Took You to the Beach for the First Time

We wrapped you
in a white blanket and walked out

to a large umbrella that sat on the edge
of the ocean. The tide was high

so the water reached the front legs
of our chair before sliding back

into its own slow, unabating arms.
I sat you between my legs on the blue

chair and drizzled sand in between
your toes and told you that this sand

was here before you and me and Grandma
and her grandma. You looked down

at your feet and looked at me and looked
up at the umbrella that kept the sun

from burning your new skin with its
dispassionate rays. It is such a simple joy

to watch you watch the world, to see you
see each thing for the first time, to watch

you feel sand on your feet but to not yet
know its name. I held you as you fell

asleep, and watched a boy run out into
the ocean and dive under a cresting wave.

I held my breath, until I saw his
head rise up on the other side.

Ode to the Bear Hug

As soon as I open the
door, I set my bag down
and crouch into the
appropriate position
and growl this guttural
invitation into my arms.
You shriek and you smile
and you move your small
feet as fast as you possibly
can in my direction, which
sometimes means you
fall, but when you
look up I am still there,
and my arms are still
open like a universe
in need of a planet
to make it worth
something. You pick
yourself back up
and your body wobbles
while you regain
your balance, and you
laugh and I laugh and your
mother looks at us
and says *my silly silly boys*
and when you finally

reach my arms I fall

back and you fall on

top of me and we roll

on the floor and I say

bear hug

bear hug

bear hug

over and over again.

For Your First Birthday

we wore party hats, ate cake, and sang
happy birthday while your mother
stood on one side and I on the other.
After the tranquil ballad concluded
everyone clapped and smiled before my
father, already shifting his knees back
and forth in anticipation of the harmonious
transition, said *one—two—one, two, three*
and on the third count every person in
the room began clapping and stepping
and dropping their shoulders while the
Stevie Wonder incarnation of the
birthday song filled the room. How
glorious a sight it is, to see an entire
room of people you love swaying in
unbridled synchronization to a song we
have transformed into tradition, a ballad
we have reimagined to help us mark this
annual celebration. Could Stevie have
imagined, back in 1980, when he
wrote this ode to Dr. King hoping it
might convince an unwilling Reagan
to make the good reverend's birthday
a holiday, that he was writing what
would become the a cappella ode

of our people? And this is what I hope
you have learned of us. That we took
this skin and transformed it into song.
That we can call for freedom and sing
sweet jubilee all in the same breath.

When We Told You Another Baby Was Coming

I'm not sure that you
understood, but I brought
your ear to your mother's
belly so you could listen
to the chorus of lightning
bugs buzzing inside. We said,
there is a baby in here and you
are going to be a big brother
and I spread my arms and said
my love for both of you is
as big as the universe. You
looked at the belly and looked
at us and spread your arms
and said *baby universe*
except *universe* sounded
like *moon horse* and you
pointed to your mother's
belly and repeated *baby moon horse*
over and over again and I smiled
and told you yes, the baby
moon horse would be here soon.

Legacy

Your maternal great-grandmother's
voice was the shade under an oak tree
and her laugh was the branch that
stretched down to let you climb it.
Your paternal great-grandfather was a fist
full of embers that never burned
the ones he loved.

Counting Descent II

My son was born on the seventy-first day
of spring on the fifth floor of a hospital
in a city with a history of burning.
He had two grandmothers in the room

and four generations in the world. My
daughter was born on the fifty-ninth day
of winter and two doors down
from the room her brother was born

in twenty-one months before. Both of my children
were induced several weeks before they were
due because waiting any longer would have
been a risk to both of their lives. I met

my wife two years, one month, and seven
days before our first child arrived and three
relationships after I assumed no one like her
existed. We sat at a table in a city 893 miles

away from where we live now for four times
longer than we planned and talked about things
we had spent half our lives attempting
to forget. When the bar closed we walked

two miles to her apartment where two dates
later we'd kiss for the first time. After
seventeen months and three doctor's
appointments we started trying to have a child

because the doctors said that we had less
than a one percent chance. I'm not sure
how they came up with that number but
I remember all the doctors kept saying

I'm sorry   I'm sorry   I'm so sorry.

Where Are They Now?

The year you were born 3,853,471
other babies were born in this country.

If my math is right that's
    10,557 every day.
        440 every hour.
            7 every minute.

I think about them sometimes, those other babies
who came into the world during that same lap
around the sun. I think of the twins born down
the hall from you with tiny hands and quiet hearts.

I think of the tubes crawling over their chests, how
they rose and fell like waves desperately grasping
for the shore.

I think of their parents, who sat beside them in
the NICU every day until the shapes of their bodies
were imprinted on the chairs, until the nurses told
them that they should go home and rest because
their little ones needed them to be strong.

I think about where those babies are now.

Do they laugh like you do?

Do they wrap their fingers around their father's thumb as they fall asleep?
Do they smile when their mother kisses their bellies?

Yesterday, we saw two twin boys in the grocery store.
They were dressed in matching striped shirts
and wearing shoes that flashed with every step.

I wondered, for a moment, if they were the boys from the NICU.
I so desperately wanted it to be them.
I so desperately wanted them to have made it home.

I Am Looking at a Photo

of George Floyd and his daughter as they sit
in the front seat of his car. The little girl is adorned
in matching mulberry-colored clothes from her shirt
to her pants, with small silver balls holding her braids
together on either side of her head. She is holding
a pair of plastic sunglasses below her face, as if she
has just taken them off to grace us with a glance,
as if the passenger seat was a red carpet and we
have all been waiting for the star to arrive. Her father
is in the foreground. Black hat, black shirt,
white pants—mouth slightly agape as if in the middle
of some utterance we'll never hear. They have
the same eyes, I think. And cheeks that blossom
like marigolds. I wonder where they were going,
or where they were coming from. Perhaps they were
just sitting there together, and after this photo
was taken she told him the joke about the banana—
you know the one. And maybe George laughed
so hard his belly hurt, and maybe she told the joke again
because she loved how her father's laugh sounded like
a carnival full of your favorite games. And maybe
things weren't always perfect, but maybe this moment
was, and maybe that's enough of a memory to hold on to.

The First Time I Saw My Grandfather Cry

was when we were waiting for news of my grandmother.
The doctor walked into the waiting
room and ushered my mother to its far corner
near the nurses' desk,
the corner with the vending machine
that was out of everything but sour skittles and snickers,
that hummed like it was trying to tell you something
but couldn't find the right words.
The doctor lowered his head and whispered to my mother.
Her hand moved
over her mouth.
The room was

quiet

but for the machine and the doctor's hand touching
the keys inside his pocket.
She walked over to my grandfather
and held both his hands in hers.
She whispered to him.
His face became a lake
after an oil spill
silent   empty   waiting
for someone to clean up the mess,
and see if anything beneath the surface
had survived.

Coming Home

This is the house I was raised in.
Sometimes I still remember how it smelled
like warm butter and cinnamon, and how the living
room glittered with sun in the early afternoons,
how jazz records spread across the kitchen and clung
to the walls of every room.

There is where I fell on my roller skates and the blood
slalomed like a red river down my leg.
There is where, after it healed, your grandfather kissed my head,
then told me to put the skates back on and keep going.

This is where your grandfather took me fishing for the first time
and a snapper almost pulled me overboard.
This is where I learned that the sky doesn't swallow the ocean.
This is where I learned that it does.

This is where your grandmother made biscuits and sacrifices.
This is where I learned that I hadn't made enough.
This is where we tried to plant a garden and nothing grew.
This is where I watched this city beg for breath.

This is where I first ate a po-boy, and the bread crumbs
tumbled down my shirt like falling stars.
This is where your great-grandmother is buried
and this is where your great-grandfather places the flowers
when he comes to tell her hello.

This restaurant used to be a barbershop
and this barbershop used to be a house.
An old woman used to live here, and every day
she would ask me where my umbrella was
even when there were no clouds in the sky,
You got to be prepared for the things you can't see, she'd say.

Cartography

It has been brought to my attention that Louisiana's coastline is eroding
so quickly that it is losing a football field of marshland every hundred
minutes. All the while the map of Louisiana has remained the same
for several decades, though if it were accurate, hundreds of
miles of land would disappear into the Gulf of Mexico.
I think about how difficult it is for any of us to
admit that we're not who we used to be.
That something in us has been lost
over time and will probably never
come back. It's so hard to
disappear without anyone
noticing. It's so hard to
be honest about the
changing contours
of your past with-
out the sky
murmuring
under its
breath.

After the Storm They Attempted to Identify the Bodies

that had been floating in the water for several weeks // their skin was not their skin anymore // their faces were no longer their faces // families attempted to identify their kin // by whatever was left // a wristwatch full of water that fogged the glass // the hands stuck on 4:42 // was it morning or late afternoon // the pair of brown leather shoes his wife had just purchased // she remembers because they were on sale that day // and afterward they went to get two scoops of ice cream // like they had when they were kids // when they knew only of love and not the heartbreak that follows // and there was the small gold cross he wore // even though he believed in no god // i mean where was god when this city was suffocated by inertia's heavy hand // what is prayer but words that always seem to drown // but he knew his wife loved to see him wearing the treasured trinket // knew that she loved the way its golden gleam kissed his skin as it bounced softly on his chest // so he left the trinket around his neck // and that's how she knew it was him // who else could it be // no // thank you // i don't need to see // his face // again // i'm sure.

For the Doctor's Records

My father has chronic kidney disease.
He has had two transplants thanks
to two people who were generous
in ways I'm worried I am not. My mother
has a nerve in her neck that doesn't let her sleep
through the night. My mother's mother died
of blood clots. My father's father died
with Alzheimer's casting a cloud
over everything inside him. My wife
had complications while she was pregnant
with both my son and daughter.
Both arrived early and I held my breath
until each of them released their first.
My wife's mother escaped a war and lived
to tell us how the memory is still
whispering inside her. I enjoy fried foods.
I eat too much salt. I worry about having more
than one drink. I've seen people in my family
become consumed by things they didn't know
could kill them. My knees hurt some days.
I feel my bones ache when it rains
like the old folks used to say.
I don't know what is in my body
and what is in my head. I want to take more
pain medicine but I'm afraid of what I can't
control. My chest gets tight when I lie

to people I love. My mother's sister had breast
cancer. My mother's brother let alcohol turn
him into silence. I remain astonished
by how cicadas live for seventeen years
underground and then die within weeks
of coming up to meet the world.

Deceit

My grandmother died over a decade ago but my grandfather's home still smells like her hair. Every pillow on the couch, every coat hanging in the closet, every book sitting on the shelf. All these years later, I still can't tell the difference between a memory and grief's imagination. Sometimes, when I sit in her chair, I imagine her saying things she never said, something that might have prepared me for her passing, something that would have made it so I didn't have to imagine her in coat pockets she never wore and behind book sleeves she never opened. Sometimes, when I sit there for too long I find myself laughing at jokes she never told, but I hear them in her voice. I eat food she never cooked but imagine her opening the oven and pulling out the broiling tray. I once heard that when an oak tree is cut down sparrows whose nest sat in its branches will find another tree and another nest and will convince themselves the eggs inside it are their own.

Expedience

When I received the call about my uncle's death,
I was sad but not surprised.

You can still mourn the damage done by a storm
even if you stood on the shore and saw it coming.

For a long time in my family, we had this habit of talking
about things without actually talking about them.

My uncle struggled for a long time with demons
we couldn't see—

see, there I go again, making another metaphor,
describing something as a monster

because I'm too scared
to call it an illness.

Removing a single brick
can cause the entire house to crumble.

A small amount of gasoline floating
atop an ocean can still start a fire.

For the Doctor's Records—Follow-Up

Not much has changed since last time.
I'm not sleeping enough.
Four or five hours a night.
My blood pressure fluctuates.
I run four times a week
but usually it's away from something.
The other day, my mother's father
didn't remember my name.
Last night my son cut his hand and cried
in a way that opened a canyon inside me.
I wrapped a bandage around his bleeding
palm and stroked his head until he fell asleep.
Last night, another boy who could have
once been me or who might one day be
my son was killed by police but this time
no cameras showed up.
I haven't cried in a long time.
There have been 11,315 sunsets
since I was born and I haven't stopped
to watch any of them.

We See Another School Shooting on the News

and I don't know how I am ever
supposed to let you
out of my sight. I think about
those children, how they woke
up and had breakfast that morning
as they did all the mornings
before: half-eaten Pop-Tarts and eggs
in a coat of ketchup. How they insisted
on wearing their favorite shirt even
though it was covered in stains.
How they tied their shoes and double
knotted them, just to be sure.
How they smiled when they saw
their friends on the bus, and told
them about the soccer game they'd had
that weekend, the goal they scored.
How none of them could have ever
known what was coming.
I fear everything I cannot control
and know that I control nothing.
I am standing in a thunderstorm
attempting to shield you from
every jagged slice of yellow sky.
I am trying to inhale all the smoke
from this burning world while
asking you to hold your breath.

The Gun

the gun heard the first shot   the gun thought it was a bursting pipe   the gun heard the second shot and the third   and the fourth   the gun realized this was not a pipe   the gun's teacher told everyone to get on the ground   the gun's teacher went to lock the door   the gun saw glass break   and the teacher slump   and bleed   and fall silent   the gun texted its parents   and said *i love you*   *i'm so sorry for any trouble i've caused all these years*   *you mean so much to me*   *i'm so sorry*   the gun thought it would never leave the classroom   the gun moved to a closet filled with several other shaking guns   the gun texted its best friends in the group chat to see if they were okay   the gun waited on a response   the gun received one   the gun did not receive another   the gun waited for an hour   the gun heard the door kicked open   the gun was still   in the closet   and didn't know who had entered the room   the gun thought this was the end   the gun thought of prom and graduation and college and children and all the things the gun would never have   the gun heard more bullets   the gun heard *he's down!*   the gun climbed out of the closet   the gun put its hands on its head   the gun walked outside   the gun saw the cameras   the gun hugged its sobbing mother   and cried into her arms   the gun heard *thoughts and prayers*   the gun heard *second amendment*   the gun heard *lone wolf*   the gun texted its friend again   the gun waited for a message   the message never came

This Year Was the First Year I Could Not Remember Your Voice

I tried to imagine the phrases only you would say,
but could only hear them falling
from someone else's lips.

I tried to imagine the stories you would tell me,
but your laugh collapsed
under the weight of this grief.

I remember the words you uttered,
but I don't remember the voice
that said them.

I remember you would call me *sugar,*
but I can't remember exactly how
the *r* melted when it met the air.

I remember how you'd tell me *be careful,*
but I am forgetting how your accent cocooned
the warning around my ears.

It's strange how I cannot remember your voice,
but if I heard it, I would immediately know
it was you.

Ode to the Double Stroller

You are the monarch of suburban pavement,
a double helix unbound and unbothered,
a map unfurling itself across the table
and pushing everything else onto the floor.
Oncoming joggers have no choice
but to step off the sidewalk to make room
for your grandeur, to genuflect at the sight
of something so worthy of a new parent's praise.
You contain multitudes—and when I say
multitudes I mean a literal cornucopia
of small items packed inside compartments
and cupholders. I mean apple slices
and sippy cups and extra diapers just in case.
I mean fruit pouches and coloring books
and an extra change of clothes.
You repository of Ritz crackers.
You collapsible companion.
You venerated vehicle.
You are the only way
I am ever able to make it
out of the house.
You are the only way the infant sleeps
and the only way the toddler will sit
down for more than three seconds.
Some say you're too unwieldy,
but your nimble rubber wheels swivel

three hundred sixty degrees on demand.

Together we dance across the concrete

while strangers look on in awe,

loose Cheerios falling

at our sides and marking

the path we've traveled.

Gold Stars

On the days when I am out alone with my children
I am made to feel as if I am a saint or a god
or the undisputed best father of all time.

What I mean is that when we walk into CVS
and my daughter is wrapped on my chest
and my son toddles at my side people stop

and look and gasp and point and walk up to me
asking to shake my hand. Men pat me on the back.
Women touch my shoulder and touch their hearts.

The manager at the front of the store comes onto
the loudspeaker to say *excuse me may I have everyone's*
attention, on aisle seven you can get three boxes of detergent

for the price of two and on aisle five there is an incredible
father running errands alone with his children.
Everyone in the store bursts into applause and someone

walks over to hand me a crown and a ribbon and a coupon
for an all-you-can-eat buffet. Just the other day, a woman
at the park told me how wonderful it is that I took the time

to babysit my children. Just the other day, I changed
a dirty diaper and someone said *praise Jesus!*
Just the other day, a man on the road stopped his car

in the middle of the street, rolled down his window
and told me I was father of the year. It's not that I don't
appreciate the sentiment it's just that this man has no idea

what kind of father I actually am. All he saw was me
and two children and a diaper bag teeming with crackers.
It's not that I don't want people to tell me

I'm doing a good job it's just I am praised for the sorts
of things no one ever thanks my wife for. I am adorned
in a garland of gold stars for simply being in this body.

Zoom School with a Toddler

Okay let's sit here and wait for your teacher to arrive yes you can have a snack no we don't have any more raisins you had them all for breakfast do you want an apple wait I think someone is here let's turn on the camera hi Ms. Maria can you hear us look it's your friend Connor son wave hello to Connor hold on don't get so close to the screen hey please don't lick the camera oh look all your friends are coming oh wow whoever that is in the corner has some great natural light damn look at the size of those windows ah right the apple let me get that no son they can't hear you right now because you're muted hold on I'll be right there now where did I put those apples hey please don't take your sister's toys while she is playing with them say sorry to your sister do you need to go sit on the stairs and take some breaths oh no not you Ms. Maria so sorry I thought we were muted okay let's watch Ms. Maria read the story wait how come no one is moving is she frozen are we frozen hello can you hear us son you don't need to yell let's restart the computer wait where did your sister go please sit still for a second did our Internet go out why are so many raisins on the floor okay your sister was behind the ottoman hey what did you just put in your mouth oh god spit that out now no not on the couch jesus let me get a napkin okay are you good let's log back in wait where did everyone go is the story done?

In the Ocean There Is a Small Jellyfish

named the *Turritopsis dohrnii* and scientists believe
it is the only creature in the world that, upon reaching
adulthood, is able to regenerate its cells and go back
to the beginning of its life cycle. Theoretically, it can do so
indefinitely which, in essence, makes the jellyfish immortal.

I think of Granddad in his chair, his blue veins growing
thick down the side of his legs, the ear he can no longer
hear out of, the way his hands shake and his spoon quivers
and his soup spills onto the table. There is no regeneration
to help his hands unlearn this trembling. I am angry with
the jellyfish for its indifferent floating through the sea.
I am angry at its cells and their self-absorbed survival.
My grandfather is eroding away and science tells me
I must accept it. What need does a jellyfish have
for an infinity that will only get lost in the current?

Ossicones

My son tells me
that his favorite animal is the giraffe.
Yesterday it was the hippopotamus.
The day before it was the zebra.
Last week it was the beluga whale.
But today it is the giraffe.
So we watch videos of this tall,
gangly creature with its long neck,
black eyes, and horns unlike any horns
we have seen before.
And my son asks me why the giraffe
has horns, and I tell him
I actually don't know,
and that when I was his age
I thought that the giraffe must have
just had an extra pair of ears.
And my son says
giraffes don't have four ears,
Daddy. That would make them aliens.
And of course he is correct, of course
these could not be ears, of course the idea
of a four-eared creature is reserved
for the extraterrestrials we imagine
when we look up to the stars.
But on the giraffe they are called *ossicones,*
though we decide to call them

horns anyway, and it turns out
they don't do much of anything but exist
as an heirloom passed down from ancestors
who had more use for these protrusions
of cartilage than their long-necked
descendants. And I look at my son,
and think of all the things I might try
to give him that he will one day have
no need for. The things that serve
no function, other than being ornaments
of a time that came before.
The things that continue to make us
who we are long after
they have served their purpose.

You Ask Me What Sounds a Giraffe Makes

I do not know the answer, but we look it up
and discover that they hum at a frequency lower
than most humans are able to hear. And you look
at me and say *but doesn't that make them sleepy?* and I do
not understand your question. I do not follow
the connection between the soft purr of this
towering creature and the onset of fatigue. I ask you
what you mean and you say *isn't humming what you
and Mommy do at bedtime?* and I smile and grab your cheek
and give praise for the way your mind works, how
your brain leaps like a field of rousing tiger
lilies on the advent of a new spring.

Yesterday Afternoon I Took You to the Park

and you love the way the flowers blossom and how the taller
they grow the more wildly they dance, how the stems become
pairs of limber hips, how the petals become a mop of hair,
how when the clouds blow over and the sun sweeps across
a bed of azaleas they glimmer like an orange ocean. And I love
how the gleam on the petals draws you in, how when you tumble
down the slide you run toward the bed of flowers and lean
over to smell them, how you look at me and say *wow!* after
the sweet scent of spring tickles your nostrils, how you proceed
to repeat that action for the next twenty flowers, how when
the wind blows and you watch the stems dance you wobble
your hips to be like the flowers, how you swing your body
so hard you fall over and begin to cry, how then you
get up and laugh and do it all over again.

The Most Remarkable Thing About Dinosaurs

Over the course of your young life I have learned
more about dinosaurs than I ever thought was possible.
Together, we've learned that the velociraptor had feathers
and was actually the size of a turkey. We've learned

that a Parasaurolophus could sing using a crest
that extended from the back of its head like a trumpet
bursting out from its skull. We've learned
that the Brontosaurus was real, then wasn't real,

then eventually was real again. Occasionally, you'll ask me
which dinosaur is my favorite and these days I say
it's the Argentinosaurus, which is reported to be the largest
dinosaur that ever lived. When it walked, they say

the earth trembled like a lost child. When it turned its body,
they say its head could cover the sun. But what I love most
about the existence of this massive, lumbering sauropod
is the remarkable fact that, for as large as it is, it is still

not larger than the largest animal alive today.
The blue whale is the size of three school buses and weighs
as much as 2,667 humans. Its heart is the size of a car,
its tongue weighs as much as an elephant. When I tell you

this, you stick out your tongue and ask me how big it is,
and I say not very big but exactly the size it should be.
You do not find this reassuring.
Today, we watched a video of a blue whale sliding

through the ocean like a ribbon blowing in wind just hard
enough to remind you that it's there. You tell me
you'd like to ride a blue whale one day, and I imagine you
exploring the shape of the sea while sitting on the back

of a creature that is the catalyst to the ocean's currents.
We can spend lifetimes looking at history to find
the most extraordinary things, when sometimes
they are right in front of us.

Ars Poetica

Before I tuck you into bed you ask me
what poets write poems about.

I tell you a poem can be
about anything.

You look around your bedroom,
eyes darting back and forth.

Can a poem be about a lamp?
Of course.

Can a poem be about a door?
Definitely.

Can a poem be about Pluto??
Many are.

So everything is a poem??
Everything.

How can everything be a poem?
Well, poems are in everything.

Poems are in... everything?
Yep.

Poems are in that cup?

Uh-huh.

Poems are in my shoe?

Indeed.

POEMS ARE INSIDE OF ME?!

They are.

You lift your pajama shirt to examine what lies beneath it,

fingers combing for evidence of the language

I told you was there. Searching for something to tell you

that you are what you have always been to me.

Above Ground

For weeks, we can't go outside without the cicadas'
song wrapping itself around the three of us like a quilt.
The tree in our front yard has become their sanctuary,
a place where they all seem to congregate

and sing their first and final songs.
We get closer, and see the way their exoskeletons
ornament the bark like golden ghosts,
shadows abandoned by their bodies

searching for new life.
One of you is four years old. One of you is two.
The next time the cicadas rise out of the earth
you will be twenty-one and nineteen.

I think of how much might change between these cycles.
How much of our planet will still be intact?
What sort of societies will the cicadas return to
when they next make their way up from the earth?

When they first arrive, you are both frightened
of this new noise that hangs in the air,
of these small orange-and-black-winged bodies
that fall from the sky like new rain.

They don't bite, I say.
But neither of you believes me.
So I reach out to one of the branches
and allow one of the orange-eyed creatures to climb

onto my finger. You both watch it roam around my hand
as it becomes familiar with the flesh of my palm,
your eyes widening at the revelation that this infrequent
visitor has no interest in piercing my skin.

And maybe that is enough, because now
you both try to pick up cicadas from the ground
and collect them in buckets as if they are treasure.
And maybe they are.

Maybe treasure is in what dies almost
as quickly as it rises from the earth.
Maybe treasure is anything that reminds you
what a miracle it is to be alive.

Tradition

On Sundays we make French toast
the way my father made French toast
with me. Each of you stand on stools

that lift your bodies above the counter
and I roll your pajama sleeves up
to your elbows then ask you

if you're ready to start. You both take turns
shouting out everything we need to begin—
an incantation of ingredients that have become

the lyrics to a song only we know. So much
of what I try to do as a father is put back together
the puzzle pieces of what my father did for me.

What is the way he held me
when I first said I was afraid of the dark?

How long did he let the silence between us sit
when I'd done something that broke his trust?

What was the shape of his eyes when he told me
he'd never be disappointed if I tried my best?

I don't always remember what he said,
but I remember how it felt to have him there,
to have his body brushing against mine

when he reached for the bread, to have
his hands wrap around my own as they guided me
in cracking the eggs, to remember how he extended

the measuring spoon full of sugar
and cinnamon toward me so that together
we could use our fingers to lick it clean.

The end products aren't exactly the same.
I don't use all the same ingredients. Sometimes
I make substitutions, sometimes I burn the bread.

Sometimes he did too.

But I try to remind myself that all these years
later, I don't remember what the bread tasted
like, just that my father had put it on my plate.

What I've Learned

I've read that humans can hold their breath for twice as long underwater
as they can on land because once submerged the body's heart rate slows
in order to conserve oxygen. Once, when I was a boy, I drifted
out past the buoys and got trapped under the current. In that moment
I thought I was going to drown, but the air held steady in my lungs
until I was able to find the surface. I live in constant awe of my body
and what it can do. I cut my hand while chopping onions and within hours
my body has reconnected the skin. My skeleton replaces itself ten times
over the course of my life and somehow it never makes a sound.
I do not make the choice to breathe, my body does it for me.
There are sixty-thousand miles of blood vessels in my body
and every single centimeter keeps me alive.

Dance Party

Sometimes in the evenings after dinner,
after the spaghetti has been slurped
and I have bribed the broccoli into their bellies,
I give both of my children . . . the look.

When my eyes meet theirs, they know what time it is.
They push in their chairs, they stretch their legs,
and we move the table to the far end of the dining room
to clear space for what we all know is coming.

Alexa, play the post-dinner dance party playlist.

And within seconds, Martha Wash's booming
voice rolls like thunder over our bodies.

Everybodyyy dance nowwww!

The electronic keyboard and the drums
meet in the middle of the room like two dinosaurs
ready to claim this kitchen as their own.
Immediately the jumping begins, and my daughter

is flinging her limbs like an off-beat octopus,
hands slapping the air behind her
as if she is trying to smack anyone
who enters her sacred space.

I turn around and my son is doing the robot…
or is being eaten by a robot…
or is trapped in a universe where robots take over
the bodies of little boys in peanut butter pajamas.

Nonetheless, there is a robot somewhere.

My children, bless them, have not yet learned
how to clap on the 2 and 4
so I laugh, but also cringe, as their small hands
make a mockery of the melody around them.

Now, halfway through the song, everyone is jumping,
and I, caught up in the ecstasy of this moment, fall
to the ground and convince this no-longer-young
body that it is a good idea to start doing the worm.

And when my children see me, their eyes become pools
of possibility, and it is clear they see this as a clarion call
to climb onto my back. And now, here we are,
this strange trifecta, this unlikely trio; a robot

and an octopus riding the back of a worm
who will certainly need some Tylenol before bed.
It is at this moment that their mother comes home.
And when she opens the door everyone is screaming,

the speakers are blasting, and the percussion is shaking every wall around us. We look up at her, and she looks down at us, and we have no explanation for this strange scene, only an invitation for her to join.

The Andromeda Galaxy Is the Closest Galaxy to Our Milky Way

and it is the most distant object visible to the naked eye.
It is 2.5 million light-years away, which means that when
we see it, we are seeing that galaxy as it was 2.5 million years
ago, long before we were ever part of this planet,

long before you came into this world like a shooting star.
We read this fact in one of your books about space
and you ask me how it's possible to see something
from so long ago, even if that thing is no longer there.

I am far from a physicist, but I do my best to explain
the speed of light by moving my hands back and forth
in front of my face as quickly as I can.
You are unconvinced by this incoherent explanation,

and now my arms are sore. So instead, what I say
is that when I look at you, it's like I am looking
at my grandmother, a woman you never met
but whose stardust is glimmering in your eyes.

When I look at you, it's like I am seeing everything
that came before, all the people I love
who once lived but who are no longer living,
all of the history that has brought you here to me.

Alarm

You were sitting at the top of the slide when
your brother yelled from the monkey bars
to watch how he could swing his body toward
the sky. After I watched him finish his playground
performance I turned back to the top of the slide
to watch you make your way down. But I didn't see you
there. My eyes widened and I scanned the playground
searching for you in a sea of other children
but I couldn't find your face. My heart began to gallop,
and whatever cool I had attempted to keep vanished
like a shadow stripped of light. I spun around
and began calling your name—a crescendo of terror
in my throat. Worst-case scenarios circled like storms
in my head. I began moving around without any idea
of where I was going. It might have been five seconds,
but in my chest it felt like forever. And then, there
you were, emerging from the other side of the swings,
holding a leaf that you told me looks like a star.
Everything in my body unclenched, grateful for a storm
that dissipated before it made contact with the shore.
I took a breath. *It does look like a star,* I said, as you
put the leaf in my hands and told me it was a gift.

Prehistoric Questions

During your bath time, each of us holds
a small plastic dinosaur engaged in battle.
Your T-Rex hides behind mountains
of suds while my Spinosaurus dips beneath
the water in preparation for a surprise attack.
After the battle has finished,
as I begin scrubbing the dirt out of your hair,
you ask me how the dinosaurs died.
I reach the washcloth behind your ears
and tell you that one day an asteroid
the size of a mountain struck the earth
which sent clouds of soot into the sky
so vast that it blocked most of the sun.
Without the sun all the plants died,
which meant all the animals that eat the plants died,
which meant all the animals that eat the animals
that eat plants died. I think this is mostly right,
but my hands are covered in bathwater
and my phone is in another room. You are silent
for a moment, and as I begin to rinse the soap
from your body, you ask me if this is how we will die
too, at the hands of a giant asteroid that comes to earth
and wipes out everything we see. I turn your body
toward me, hold your shoulders in my hands,
and tell you that no asteroid will be coming to earth
anytime soon. I speak with a certainty I do not have.

I reassure you with language that floats away
as soon as it leaves my lips. I lift you from the tub,
wrap a towel around you, and you ask me how
we will die. I pause. I feel my heart tremble
with all the answers I do not have. Part of me
wants to say something about heaven and angels
and forever. Part of me wants to say something
about how life one day ending makes the whole thing
so worth living. I realize how unprepared I am to talk
to you about how this will all end for us,
and how precarious and uncertain
our time on this fragile planet is. I tell you
that the hope is for all of us to live for a very long time,
which is why you need to eat your carrots. I don't know
if that was the right thing to say, but at that moment it was
all I had. You squinch your nose and say *carrots yuck,*
as I rub the towel over your wet curls and kiss your head.

Punctuation

I went to the store filled with water.

I went to the store, filled with water.

The store is submerged

or

I am crying in the aisles

There is something in your eyes I can't get out.

There is something in your eyes; I can't get out.

I am trying to help

or

I am trying to run away

I am scared you don't really know me.

I am scared; you don't really know me.

I am expressing concern about where we're going

or

I am making a declaration of where we are

The wind carried my mother's voice away after the storm came.

The wind carried my mother's voice away; after, the storm came.

My mother is grieving all that she lost

or

I am grieving the loss of my mother

There are new flowers on the trees I climbed every day as a child.

There are new flowers on the trees; I climbed every day as a child.

I am relishing the cycle of renewal

or

I am lamenting that something has taken my place

It's hard for me to say I am not always the man I want to be.

It's hard for me to say; I am not always the man I want to be.

I am trying to be honest with myself

or

I am trying to be honest with you.

Univers(al)

My son is obsessed with space. Hanging on the wall
of his bedroom is a poster of the solar system. The sun
sits at the center. Each of the eight planets
encircles the yellow-orange orb, their respective orbits
depicted by thin white lines that make it look
as if each is being held up in the universe by a string.
When he eats a Ritz he uses his teeth to carve the cracker
into a crescent moon, then holds it above his head
as if the sky might reach down to scoop it in its starlit hands.
He dreams of being an astronaut (and a teacher and chef
and a superhero and a Pokémon) and I dream
of his dreams and how possible I want them all to be.

Ode to Bedtime

after the teeth have been brushed
and the stories have been read,
after the night-light flickers on
and radiates from the corner
of your room and the fan warbles
its song of white noise, after I have
asked you one last time if you need
to use the bathroom and after you say
no but I tell you to try one more time
anyway, after the last sip of water
has disappeared behind your lips
and our prayers decrescendo toward
a secret, after I have rubbed your belly
and kissed your head and told you
that a million trips to the moon and back
are still not enough to match
the way you make my heart burst open
with a gratitude I have never known,
after I shut the door that always creaks
right before it reaches the frame and after
I have turned the knob so that the latch
bolt slides into place with a quiet click,
I stand there for a minute and wait
to see if you have settled into slumber,
then walk downstairs and collapse

into the couch, exhausted, but thankful

for these moments that I know I'll miss

when they are gone.

Ode to Those First Fifteen Minutes After the Kids Are Finally Asleep

Praise the couch that welcomes you back into its embrace
as it does every night around this time. Praise the loose
cereal that crunches beneath your weight, the whole-grain
golden dust that now shimmers on the backside of your pants.
Praise the cushion, the one in the middle that sinks like a lifeboat
leaking air, and the ottoman covered in crayon stains that you
have now accepted as aesthetic. Praise your knees, and the evening
respite they receive from a day of choo-choo-training along the carpet
with two eager passengers in tow. Praise the silence, oh the silence,
how it washes over you like a warm bedsheet. Praise the walls
for the way they stand there and don't ask for anything.
Praise the seduction of slumber that tiptoes across your eyelids,
the way it tempts you to curl up right there and drift away
even though it's only 7:30 p.m. Praise the phone you scroll through
without even realizing that you're scrolling, praise the video
you scroll past of the man teaching his dog how to dance merengue,
praise the way it makes you laugh the way someone laughs
when they are so tired they don't know if they will ever stand
up again. Praise the toys scattered across the floor, and the way you
wonder if it might be okay to just leave them there for now,
since you know tomorrow they will end up there again.

When Standing in a Cabin at the Whitney Plantation

I close my eyes and consider for a moment what it would mean
to fall asleep in my home, to wake up, and to find my children
gone. To not know where they were. To not know who had
taken them. To not know if I would see them again. I open
my eyes and watch flecks of sun trickle in through
an unsteady roof above me and listen to the sound
of wooden planks made from cypress trees groaning underfoot.
I consider that this was the omnipresent peril that millions
of enslaved people lived under. I consider how it wasn't
so long ago. How the threat of being separated
from those you love hung over every second of their lives.
I shudder tracing the contours of this possibility. I lose
my breath imagining just how quickly a body can disappear.

Look at That Pond

Look at the fish swimming under its silver surface. Look how the surface shimmers like sound. Look how the fish follow one another, how their bodies bend like strings of a harp. Look how this stone skips staccato across the surface then disappears with a whisper. Look how the ripples in the water never seem to stop. Look at the way the colors of the fish's scales change as the sun slides across the sky. Look at the way the plants surround the pond as if they were trying to keep it safe. One day this pond will become a swamp and this swamp will become a marsh and this marsh will become a forest. Maybe one day my children's children's children will walk around in this forest and find the stone we skipped. A single fish can lay over one million eggs in a single year. Tiny plankton in bodies of water like this one produce over half of the oxygen on earth. My life is made possible by trillions of tiny mysteries. I exist because of so many things I'll never see.

Acknowledgments

Thank you to the literary journals and magazines that have published previous versions of these poems:

Academy of American Poets—"FaceTime"
The Adroit Journal—"Here Nor There"
Auburn Avenue—"This Year Was the First Year I Could Not Remember Your Voice"
Harvard Kennedy School Journal of African American Public Policy—"Your National Anthem"
New York Times Magazine—"And the World Keeps Spinning" and "At the Superdome After the Storm Has Passed"
POETRY—"The Drone"
The Rumpus — "Pangaea"
Sierra—"Above Ground"
Southern Indiana Review—"For the Doctor's Records"
Wildness—"When People Say 'We Have Made It Through Worse Before,'" "Waiting on a Heartbeat," and "The *New York Times* Reports That 200 Civilians Have Just Been Killed by U.S. Military Air Strikes"

Thank you to the entire team at Little, Brown for putting together this book with such care.

Thank you to my agent, Alia Hanna Habib, for always being in my corner.

Thank you to Safia Elhillo and Elizabeth Acevedo for your edits, your eyes, and your friendship.

Thank you to Jorie Graham for your guidance and your belief.

Thank you to all the writers who came before me whose work makes my own possible.

Thank you to all the writers who have come up alongside me for being constant sources of inspiration.

Thank you to my parents, for a lifetime of support.

Thank you to my children: this book was written about you, for you, and with you.

Thank you to Ariel: you are the center of my universe.

Notes

"Nomenclature" is written after a poem by Safia Elhillo.

"The *New York Times* Reports That 200 Civilians Have Just Been Killed by U.S. Military Air Strikes" is written after a poem by Hanif Abdurraqib.

"This Is an Incomprehensive List of All the Reasons I Know I Married the Right Person" is written after a poem by Matthew Olzmann.

"Coming Home" is written after a poem by Tyree Daye.

"For the Doctor's Records" and "For the Doctor's Records—Follow-Up" are written after a poem by Nicole Sealey.

"Ode to Those First Fifteen Minutes After the Kids Are Finally Asleep" is written after a poem by Nate Marshall.

"In the Ocean There Is a Small Jellyfish" and "Nociception" are inspired by the work of Ed Yong.

The translations in "Nomenclature" are approximations, as many Igbo words cannot be translated directly into English.

About the Author

Clint Smith is the author of the narrative nonfiction book *How the Word Is Passed: A Reckoning with the History of Slavery Across America*, which was a #1 *New York Times* bestseller, the winner of the National Book Critics Circle Award for Nonfiction, and selected by the *New York Times* as one of the ten best books of 2021. He is also the author of the poetry collection *Counting Descent*, which won the 2017 Literary Award for Best Poetry Book from the Black Caucus of the American Library Association. He is a staff writer at *The Atlantic.*